Expository Nuggets
for
Today's Christians

Expository Nuggets *for* Today's Christians

Stuart Briscoe Expository Outlines

D. Stuart Briscoe

Baker Books

A Division of Baker Book House Co
Grand Rapids, Michigan 49516

© 1994 by D. Stuart Briscoe

Published by Baker Books
a division of Baker Book House Company
P.O. Box 6287, Grand Rapids, MI 49516-6287

ISBN: 0-8010-1062-4

Second printing, December 1994

Printed in the United States of America

Contents

Part 3: What's the Difference?

Part 4: Christians Awake!

Part 5: Problem Areas

Preface

Outlines and skeletons are quite similar. Sermons without outlines tend to "flop around" like bodies without bones. But bones without flesh are not particularly attractive; neither are outlines without development. The outlines presented in this book are nothing more than skeletal for a very good reason. I have no desire to produce ready-made sermons for pastors who need to develop their own, but on the other hand I recognize that many busy pastors who find sermon preparation time hard to come by may at least use them as a foundation for their own study, meditation, and preaching. They can add flesh to the bones, they can add development to structure. All the sermons based on these outlines have been preached during the last twenty-two years of my ministry at Elmbrook Church in Milwaukee, Wisconsin, and as one might expect, they vary in style and substance—not to mention quality! I trust, however, that they all seek to teach the Word and apply it to the culture to which they were preached, and if they help another generation of preachers as they "preach the Word," I will be grateful.

Part 1

What Makes Christians Tick?

1

The Gratitude Attitude

1 Corinthians 15:10

Behind every human action lies a motivation. Christian motivation is of great interest to us, but what is it? And how does it work? Paul gives us some helpful insights into his own motivation, with particular regard to the grace of God.

I. The grace of God—a divine attitude
   A. Paul's testimony
      1. By the grace of God I am what I am
      2. I am an apostle
      3. I am an "abortion"
      4. Grace is God's taking an abortion and making him an apostle
   B. Our experience
      1. We are moral failures
      2. God is absolutely just
      3. We are incapable of changing ourselves or God

    4. God is free to deal with us as he chooses
    5. He has chosen to mingle justice with mercy and grace
      a. Justice gives me what I deserve
      b. Mercy does not give me all I deserve
      c. Grace gives me what I don't deserve
    6. All this is operative "in Christ"

II. The grace of God—a dynamic stimulus
    A. His grace was not without effect
    B. The proof—I worked harder than them all
    C. *Gratia* (Lat. for "grace") is the root of gratitude
    D. Gratitude is expressed by doing God's will enthusiastically

III. The grace of God—a daily enabling
    A. Not I—but grace working alongside
    B. *Charis* (Gk. for "grace") is the root of charisma and charismata
    C. Grace gives the gift of the Spirit
    D. The Spirit brings the gifts of the Spirit
    E. All these work to equip God's people for God's calling

2

The Servant Spirit

Acts 13:36

Jesus said that he had not come to be served but to serve. His followers have been commanded to emulate his example, but developing a servant spirit does not come naturally.

I. The development of a servant spirit
   A. Service—the Christian's calling
      1. Serving the living God (1 Thess. 1:9)
      2. Serving the Christian community (Gal. 5:13)
      3. Serving the needy world (Phil. 2:22)
   B. Service—the Christian's choice
      1. Overcoming negative forces
         a. Arrogance (Phil. 2:7)
         b. Ambition (Matt. 20:24–27)
         c. Apathy (Rom. 13:11–12)

    2. Observing positive factors
      a. A sense of privilege (Acts 27:23)
      b. A sense of responsibility (Col. 3:24)

II. The channeling of a servant spirit
  A. The eternal plan of God
  B. The general plan of God
  C. The individual plan of God
    1. The uniqueness of you as a person
      a. Gifts
      b. Heritage
      c. Experience
      d. Position
    2. The uniqueness of your opportunity:
       "There's a work for Jesus only you can do"

III. The application of a servant spirit
  A. Each generation is responsible for its own
    generation
  B. This generation is responsible for this
    generation
    1. The magnitude of the task
    2. The magnificence of the opportunity
  C. Each believer is responsible for his life now
    1. Discovering your place
    2. Discharging your responsibility

IV. The results of a servant spirit
  A. Like David we will "fall asleep"
  B. Then we will face the eternal aspects of our
    service
    1. The thrill of recognition (Matt. 25:21)
    2. The certainty of reward (2 Cor. 5:10)
    3. The discovery of repercussions

3

When Duty Calls

1 Corinthians 9:1-23

Motives make people act. Motivation urges people to achieve things they consider significant. The call to duty has always been powerful for some people, but for the Christian it has special importance.

I. Rights
   A. Rights must be recognized
      1. The right to be recognized (vv. 1–2)
      2. The right to be respected (vv. 3–5)
      3. The right to be refreshed (v. 4)
      4. The right to be remunerated (vv. 7–12)
   B. Rights must be regulated
      1. Rights are secondary to responsibilities (see Exod. 20)
      2. Rights are met when responsibilities are fulfilled
      3. Rights are always subject to restraint (1 Cor. 9:15)

II. Responsibilities
   A. The reality of the law of sin and death (Rom. 8:2)
   B. The release of the Spirit of life
   C. The result of the law of Christ (1 Cor. 9:21)
      1. A deep sense of compulsion (v. 16; Matt. 14:22)
      2. A real sense of accountability (1 Cor. 9:16)
      3. A keen sense of reward (v. 17)
      4. A fine sense of trust (v. 17)

III. Results
   A. Durability
      1. Suffering when you don't have to (v. 12)
      2. Serving when you don't want to (v. 17)
   B. Expendability
      1. Saying no to a selfish role (v. 18)
      2. Saying yes to a serving role (v. 19)
   C. Flexibility
      1. In attitude —"all men" (v. 22)
      2. In approach—"all means"
      3. In action—"all things"

4
A Sense of Privilege
1 Corinthians 4:1-5

Give some people a uniform and they will be motivated. Give others a title and the same thing happens. Take others into your confidence and they will be encouraged to perform better. It all has to do with a sense of privilege.

I. A sense of privilege (vv. 1–2)
    A. A matter of position
        1. Servants of Christ
            a. *Hupēretēs* (Gk.)–"one who assists the principal in completing a task"
            b. An under-rower
            c. Pulling on an oar while Jesus charts the course
        2. Stewards of the mysteries
            a. Mysteries–the revelation of what was previously hidden
            b. Revelation contrasted with speculation
            c. The privilege of being initiated while living among the uninitiated

    B. A matter of pride
       1. Proud to be called
       2. Proud to be trusted
       3. Anxious to be found faithful

II. A feeling of pressure (v. 3)
    A. Identifying the pressure points
       1. Pressure from Christian community
          a. Manipulation–ties your hands
          b. Adulation–swells your head
          c. Confrontation–breaks your heart
       2. Pressure from outside sources
          a. Human court–literally, "man's day"
          b. Secular society and its contemporary outlook
       3. Pressure from personal expectations
          a. Unrealistically high
          b. Unforgivably low
    B. Nullifying the pressure points
       1. Discounting much of the pressure
          a. Uninformed
          b. Unhelpful
       2. Discontinuing much of the pressure
          a. Inaccurate
          b. Difficulty of establishing criteria
       3. Discover the real pressure point
          a. "It is the Lord who judges me" (v. 4)

III. A matter of perspective (vv. 4–5)
    A. It is the Lord who gave me this privileged position
    B. It is the Lord who will ultimately evaluate my performance
    C. It is the Lord who knows my motives
    D. Therefore it is the Lord I will serve until I meet him

5

A Touch of Compassion

Luke 10:30-37

Peter Ustinov said, "Charity is more common than compassion because charity is tax deductible, while compassion is merely time-consuming." His skeptical observation points out the importance of proper Christian motivation.

I. Compassion as part of the divine nature
   Note: *Compassion*—"to love, pity, show mercy, gut feeling, suffer with"
   A. God's compassion—the basis of his covenant
      1. God's call to Moses (Exod. 3:7–10)
      2. God's reminder to Moses (Exod. 34:5–7)
   B. God's compassion—the reason for Israel's survival
      1. The prophets' reiteration (Isa. 14:1)
      2. The believers' comfort (Lam. 3:21–27)
   C. God's compassion—the motive of salvation
      1. The mercies of God (Rom. 12:1–2)

   D. God's compassion–the model of Christ
      1. Demonstrated in attitude (Matt. 9:36;
         14:14)
      2. Articulated in teaching (Matt. 18:23–35)

II. Compassion as part of Christian motivation
   A. How is compassion generated? (Ps. 14:1–7)
      1. By understanding the human condition
         a. Human foolishness (v. 1)
         b. Human fallenness (vv. 1–3)
         c. Human filthiness (v. 3)
         d. Human forgetfulness (v. 4)
         e. Human fearfulness (v. 5)
      2. By recognizing the human potential
         a. Capable of being a divine residence
            (v. 5)
         b. Capable of knowing the divine presence
            (v. 6)
   B. How is compassion expressed?
      1. By a yearning heart (v. 7)
      2. By an active participation (Luke 10:30–37)
   C. Where is compassion directed?
      1. Wherever human need is in evidence (Prov.
         19:17)
      2. Wherever the opportunity is presented
         (1 John 3:16–17)

6

Team Spirit

1 Corinthians 12:1–31

Those who have participated in team activities know the value of team spirit. The French call it *esprit de corps*– "body spirit"–an expression which transfers easily to the church, the body of Christ.

I. How to generate team spirit in the church
    A. Emphasize our common experience
        1. The activity of God (v. 6)
        2. The acknowledgment of Christ (vv. 3, 5)
        3. The action of the Spirit (vv. 3–4)
           a. Baptism of the Spirit (v. 13)
           b. Indwelling of the Spirit (v. 13)
           c. Enabling of the Spirit (v. 11)
    B. Emphasize the common good (v. 7)
        1. The uniqueness of the individual
           a. Unique circumstances (v. 13)
           b. Unique calling (v. 18)
           c. Unique capability (v. 11)

    2. The importance of the body (v. 27)
      a. Interrelated (vv. 14–17)
      b. Interdependent (v. 21)
  C. Emphasize the common objective
    1. To be the body of Christ
      Note: "so also is Christ" (v. 12)
    2. The visible expression of the invisible
    3. The tangible expression of the intangible
    4. The physical vehicle of the spiritual

II. How to demonstrate team spirit in the church
  A. By demonstrating the unity of the Spirit
    1. Unity allowing diversity
      a. The same Spirit (v. 4)
      b. The same Lord (v. 5)
      c. The same God (v. 6)
    2. Diversity protecting unity
      a. Different gifts (v. 4)
      b. Different ministries (v. 5)
      c. Different workings (v. 6)
  B. By demonstrating respect for the members
    1. The less visible may be the more vital (v. 23)
    2. The less noteworthy may be the more
      necessary (v. 22)
  C. By demonstrating care for the body
    1. The unacceptability of schism (v. 25)
    2. The agony of suffering (v. 26)
    3. The empathy of success (v. 26)

III. How to perpetuate team spirit in the church
  A. By waging war on ignorance (v. 1)
    1. Objective factors
    2. Perspective factors
    3. Subjective factors
  B. By showing the more excellent way (v. 31)

7

The Fear of the Lord

2 Corinthians 5:9-21

The history of mankind will probably show that no people has ever risen above its religion, and man's spiritual history will positively demonstrate that no religion has ever been greater than its idea of God."

A. W. Tozer

I. The meaning of the fear of the Lord
   A. An accurate understanding (Prov. 9:10)
      1. Of God
         a. His holiness
         b. His righteousness
         c. His grace
      2. Of ourselves (2 Cor. 5:19–21)
         a. Our sin
         b. Our estrangement
         c. Our accountability
      3. Of reality (v. 17)
         a. Human lostness
         b. Human opportunity

   B. An appropriate response
       1. The response of reverence (Isa. 6:1–8)
           a. Smallness in the presence of immensity
           b. Silence in the presence of authority
           c. Shame in the presence of purity
       2. The response of repentance (Ps. 36:1)
           a. The detection of sin
           b. The rejection of sin
           c. The deflation of self
       3. The response of renewal
           a. A renewed desire to learn (Ps. 34:11)
           b. A renewed willingness to choose
               (Prov. 1:29)
           c. A renewed ability to evaluate (16:6)
           d. A renewed readiness to persevere
               (23:17)

II. The motivation of the fear of the Lord
     A. It leads to disciplined living
         1. Keeping his commandments (Deut. 6:2)
         2. Keeping from sinning (Exod. 20:20)
         3. Keeping from irresponsibility (2 Chron.
             19:7–9)
     B. It leads to holy living
         1. New aspirations (2 Cor. 7:1)
         2. New selectivity (6:14–18)
     C. It leads to concerned living
         1. Concern for people's spiritual well-being
             (5:11)
         2. Concern for your own integrity (1 Peter
             3:15)
     D. It leads to corporate living
         1. Submissive attitudes (Eph. 5:21)
         2. Cooperative actions (Acts 9:31)

8

Keeping On Keeping On

2 Corinthians 4:1-18

In times when people talk a lot about "burn out," it is good to remember the sentiments expressed in an old hymn: "Let me burn out for Thee, Dear Lord." Paul's life and teaching illustrate his attitude with great clarity.

I. The reality of Paul's lifestyle (vv. 8–10; 6:4–5)
   A. Pressed but not crushed (4:8)
      1. Safety blitz—not sacked
      2. Damascus (Acts 9:25)
      3. Jerusalem (Acts 23:23–24)
   B. Stretched but not snapped (2 Cor. 4:8)
      1. Rubber-band syndrome
      2. For example, 2 Corinthians 1:8–9
   C. Hounded but not abandoned (2 Cor. 4:9)
      1. For example, Philippi, Thessalonica, Berea (Acts 17:1–13)
   D. Down but not counted out (2 Cor. 4:9)
      1. For example, Iconium, Lystra, Derbe (Acts 14:1–20)

E. Pressure of circumstances (2 Cor. 6:4; see
   11:23–28)
   1. Troubles–physical, mental, spiritual
   2. Hardships–problems without solutions
   3. Distresses–locked in situations
F. Pressure from opponents (6:5)
G. Pressure of work (6:5)

II. The reaction of Paul
   A. We do not lose heart (4:1, 16)
   B. We endure all things (6:4)

III. The reasoning of Paul
   A. A feel for God's mercy (4:1)
      1. Ministry has been received
      2. Message has been recognized (3:7–18)
         a. Compared to message of Sinai
         b. Embraced in all its glory
      3. Miracle has been experienced (4:6)
         a. God has shone in our hearts
   B. A concern for Christ's honor
      Note: "For Jesus' sake" (vv. 5, 11)
      1. Servants for his sake (v. 5)
      2. Suffering for his sake (v. 11)
   C. A sense of eternal realities (vv. 16–18)
      1. Troubles achieve glory
      2. Seen things are temporary
      3. Unseen things are eternal
   D. A vision of human need (vv. 3–4)
      1. Evil activity
      2. Human blindness
      3. Perishing humanity
   E. A commitment to God's glory (v. 7)
      1. Human frailty shows off divine power
      2. Human insignificance shows off divine glory

Read Paul's summary: 2 Timothy 4:7–8.

9

For the Love of Christ

2 Corinthians 5:14-21

The thing that sets Christian motivation apart from other motivational factors is the uniqueness of the Christian's relationship with Christ. This is no more clearly exhibited than in the love relationship.

I. Recognizing the love of Christ
   A. What does Paul mean?
      1. Subjective?–Christ's love for man
      2. Objective?–man's love for Christ
      3. Context implies former; both are interrelated
   B. What does Paul understand?
      1. The human condition
        a. Sinfulness
        b. Estrangement
      2. The human need
        a. Reconciliation
        b. Justification

      3. The divine initiative
        a. Christ has died for sin
        b. Reconciliation has been made possible
        c. Man can be made righteous
      4. The divine appeal
        a. Be reconciled to God
        b. Everything is ready–only response is necessary
      5. The divine motivation
        a. The love of Christ
        b. Shown in being made sin
        c. Shown in death on a cross
  C. What does Paul conclude?
      1. The old has gone–we died with him
      2. The new has come–we live for him
      3. We are new creations in Christ

II. Responding to the love of Christ
  A. This love compels us
      1. What does compel mean?
        a. See Acts 7:57; Philippians 1:23; Luke 22:63
        b. A moral demand to respond
      2. What are we compelled to do?
        a. To love the Christ without whom we are lost
        b. To love those who without Christ are lost

III. Reflecting the love of Christ
  A. Discerning the love of Christ
      1. What I was without it
      2. What I am with it

  B. Desiring the love of Christ
      1. Appreciating its beauty
      2. Longing for its reproduction
      3. Responding to the Spirit
  C. Deciding the love of Christ
      1. It will be my constant theme
      2. It will be my continual choice

Part **2**

Real People in an Unreal World

10

What Do Real Men Eat?

Matthew 3:1-17

We *know* they don't eat quiche—but what do they eat? And who are these real men? The question, which is on many lips, suggests some degree of uncertainty. Jesus *knew* a real man when he saw one—and he knew what he ate! (see Matt. 3:4; 11:11).

I. Real men have sincerity and simplicity
  A. Sincerity attested to by
    1. Crowds (v. 5)
    2. Herod (Mark 6:20)
    3. Disciples (Mark 6:29)
    4. Jesus (Matt. 11:11)
  B. Simplicity demonstrated by
    1. A disciplined lifestyle
      a. Prayer and fasting (Luke 5:33)
      b. Locusts and wild honey (Matt. 3:4; cf. 11:18–19)
    2. A direct message
      a. Concerning the kingdom (3:1–3)
      b. Concerning the King (vv. 11–12)

    c. Concerning the people
      (1) A call to repentance
      (2) A call to confession (v. 6)
      (3) A call to conversion (Luke 3:10–14)

II. Real men have courage and conviction
  A. Convictions about
    1. Reality–water and fire (Luke 3:16)
    2. Hypocrisy–Pharisees and Sadducees (vv. 7–8)
    3. Integrity–reeds and fine clothes (Matt. 11:7–9)
    4. Purity–Herod and Herodias (14:3–4)
  B. Courage shown in
    1. Confrontation of evil
    2. Specification of good
    3. Clarification of righteousness

III. Real men have vision and vulnerability
  A. The vision of a prophet–a seer
    1. He could see what was coming
    2. He could announce who had come
  B. The vulnerability of an honest man
    1. The vulnerability of humility
      a. I must decrease–he must increase (John 3:30)
      b. I am not (John 1:19–22)
      c. I am a voice–he is the Word (John 1:23)
      d. I am a lamp–he is the Light (John 5:35)
    2. The vulnerability of honesty (Luke 7:18–20)
      a. Being honest about doubt
      b. Being honest to friends
      c. Being honest to the Lord

Points to ponder: Do we define a real man in these terms? If not, where do we get our ideas of manhood? If so, how do we develop these characteristics?

11

What Are Real Marriages Made Of?

Mark 10:6-9

Never a wedding goes by without someone saying, "Marriages are made in heaven." If they are, why do so many fail? What are real marriages made of? Jesus had some thoughts on the subject.

I. Marriage is a divine institution (v. 6)
   A. Creation ordinance contrasted with later legislation
   B. Divinely instituted for psychological reasons
      1. The need for love
      2. The need to love
   C. Divinely instituted for sociological reasons
      1. The basis of the family
      2. The family is the base of society
   D. Divinely instituted for theological reasons
      1. A model of the covenant (Jer. 2:2)
      2. A model of Christ and the church (Eph. 5:21–33)

II. Marriage recognizes divinely ordained sexuality
    (Mark 10:6)
    A. Sexuality as stated in Scripture
    B. Sexuality as modified by tradition
    C. Sexuality as radicalized in contemporary
       thinking

III. Marriage requires a willing "leaving" (v. 7)
     A. Marriage introduces a new priority
     B. Marriage demands an element of sacrifice

IV. Marriage presupposes an attitude of "cleaving" (v. 7)
    A. The bedrock of marriage is commitment
    B. The superstructure on commitment is mature
       living

V. Marriage creates a unique entity (v. 8)
   A. Two are made one
   B. God does it
   C. The one incorporates the qualities of the two
   D. The new is greater than the sum of its parts
   E. This oneness requires adjustment for life

VI. Marriage imposes a profound responsibility (v. 9)
    A. If God created it . . .
    B. We should do nothing to destroy it . . .
    C. But give ourselves to promoting and pre-
       serving . . .
    D. That which God ordained

12

Do Real Husbands Change Diapers?

Ephesians 5:1-33

At first sight the question may seem inappropriate, but further reflection shows that many questions are circulating about the part that "real husbands" play in developing "real marriages." Once again we turn to Scripture.

I. The husband as "holy" (v. 3)
    A. Holy means living in love (vv. 1–2)
        1. Because we are "dearly loved children"
        2. Because we experienced Christ's sacrificial love
    B. Holy means living in the light (vv. 8–10)
        1. Rejecting darkness
        2. Reflecting goodness, righteousness, and truth
        3. Respecting the Lord's wishes
    C. Holy means living in the Lord (vv. 15–21)
        1. Being filled with the Spirit (v. 18)
            a. Understanding (v. 17)
            b. Speaking (v. 19)

    c. Singing (v. 19)
    d. Thanking (v. 20)
    e. Submitting (v. 21)
  2. Everything in the name of the Lord
    a. In marked contrast to the surrounding society
    b. The common factors in Roman, Greek, and Jewish thought

II. The husband as "head"
  A. Contemporary usage of head
    1. Concept of authority, and so forth
    2. Consideration of Genesis 3:16
  B. Biblical usage of head
    1. Example of Christ as head of the church
      a. The source of life and blessing (Col. 3:19)
      b. The integrating factor (Eph. 4:16)
      c. The Savior of the body (Eph. 5:23)
      d. The Lord of the church (v. 24)
      e. The Lover of the bride (v. 25)
    2. The application to the husband
      a. In provision
      b. In coordination
      c. In protection
      d. In direction
      e. In sacrifice

III. The husband as "heir" (1 Peter 3:7)
  A. The husband as heir of life
  B. The wife as coheir
  C. The "considerate" factor
  D. The "respect" factor

Notes:

1. This teaching was a radical departure from established norms

2. The power was in the hands of the husbands to use or abuse
3. The Christian message brought fresh life to all
4. In what way do husbands need to apply these things today?

13

Is the Real-Women Issue Mystique or Mistake?

Luke 10:38–42

When Betty Friedan wrote, "The problem for women today is not sexual but a problem of identity, a stunting or evasion of growth that is perpetuated by the feminine mystique," she fired a shot heard around the world. To what extent was her mystique a mistake? To what extent was she right?

I. Woman's identity–revealed in creation
  A. Man–male and female (Gen. 1:26–31)
    1. Woman as created being (v. 27)
    2. Woman as bearer of divine image (v. 27)
      a. Male and female attributes of deity?
      b. Male and female models of Trinity?
    3. Woman blessed by God (v. 28)

        4. Woman commissioned by God (v. 28)
          a. To propagate the race
          b. To rule over creation
    B. Woman–man's "helpmeet" (Gen. 2:18–25)
        1. Woman made for man (v. 18)
          a. Helper (Heb., *'ezer*–see also Deut. 33:7, 26, 29)
          b. Suitable–ideal partner
        2. Woman made from man (Gen. 2:22–23)
          a. In contrast to everything made from ground (vv. 7, 9, 19)
          b. Named woman

II. Woman's identity–obscured in the fall
    A. Woman's deception (Gen. 3:1–13)
        1. Interested in "good," "pleasure," and "wisdom"
        2. Introduced to idea that these were available, independent of God
        3. Involved in debate and deception with the serpent
    B. Woman's destiny (Gen. 3:14–24)
        1. Mankind's introduction to death
        2. Woman's experience of suffering (v. 16)
        3. Woman's experience of subjugation (v. 16)
          a. Patriarchal polygamy
          b. Statements of church fathers (e.g., Tertullian and Aquinas)
          c. Attitudes of pagan philosophers (e.g., Aristotle)
          d. Prejudicial practices of world religions (e.g., Buddhism, Islam, Hinduism, Judaism, and Christianity)
        4. Woman's place in redemption (v. 15)

III. Woman's identity–renewed in redemption
   A. The promise of the new covenant (Acts 2:17–18)
      1. Women equal partners in blessing and opportunity
   B. The statement of Christian liberty (Gal. 3:28)
      1. In Christ there is a new identity
      2. This identity transcends barriers and unites in new life
      3. This experience of justification is to be worked out in relationships
   C. The treatment of women by Christ contrary to cultural norms
      1. He used women as examples of righteousness (e.g., Luke 18:1–8; 21:1–4)
      2. He shared with women of doubtful reputation (e.g., Luke 7:36–50)
      3. He honored women with responsible opportunities (e.g., John 4:39–42; 20:18)
   D. The restriction of women by apostles
      1. The "silence" restriction (1 Cor. 14:26–40)
      2. The "subordination" restriction (1 Tim. 2:11–15)
      3. The "submission" restriction (Eph. 5:21–24)

14

Do Real Families Stay Together?

Genesis 27:1–46

The family, God's basic ordained societal unit, can be an environment of great delight or the scene of intolerable stress and strain. Isaac's family knew both experiences, and a study of it may prove valuable to all those who take the family seriously.

I. How arc families founded?
   A. A marriage made with care (Gen. 24)
      1. Clearly defined principles
         a. Knowing the will of God
         b. Obeying the commands of God
         c. Trusting the guidance of God
      2. Clearly stated commitment
         a. The challenge to be committed
         b. The choice to be committed
      3. Clearly expressed love
         a. Unafraid to love
         b. Unashamed to express it

  B. Children bathed in prayer (Gen. 25)
      1. Isaac's prayer of request
          a. Children are a gift from the Lord
          b. Parents are stewards before the Lord
      2. Rebekah's prayer of anguish
          a. Insight into God's purposes
          b. Insight into her children

II. Why do families fail?
  A. The nature of a family's failure
      1. An atmosphere of intrigue
          a. Scheming instead of supporting
          b. Lying instead of loving
          c. Competing instead of complementing
      2. An attitude of indifference
          a. To an old man's infirmity
          b. To a young man's limitations
          c. To matters of integrity
          d. To matters of decency
  B. The causes of a family's failure
      1. The father
          a. Disregarded divine revelation (Gen. 25:23)
          b. Depended on natural considerations
          c. Discounted solemn oath (v. 33)
          d. Displayed prejudicial attitudes (v. 28)
      2. The mother
          a. Dedicated to her own ends
          b. Operated to her own advantage
          c. Humiliated her own husband
          d. Manipulated her own sons
      3. The sons
          a. Esau lacked any sense of priorities
          b. Jacob lacked any sense of principle

III. When do families flourish?
 A. When the father acts as head
 B. When the mother adds support
 C. When the children afford respect
 D. When the family affirms itself
 E. When the Lord approves his blessing

15

Are Real Singles Complete People?

I Corinthians 7; Matthew 19:12

Societal structures are changing dramatically in the United States; not least in the area of "singles"–those who are not married, either by choice or chance. For example, single households have increased 66 percent from 1960 to 1980. What is the status of the single person according to Scripture?

   I. Singleness and the Scriptures
      A. Some famous singles
         1. Jesus
         2. Paul
         3. Adam
         4. Anna
      B. Some famous statements
         1. "It is not good for man to be alone" (Gen. 2:18)
            a. Coupleness ordained by God
            b. Marriage normative in creation
            c. Heterosexual relationships imperative

    2. "It is not good to marry" (Matt. 19:10–12)
      a. Jesus' high standards
      b. Disciples' amazed reactions
      c. Singleness (celibacy) is a gift
      d. People are single for different reasons
    3. "It is good not to marry" (1 Cor. 7:1–9, 25–38)
      a. Singleness is a high calling (v. 7)
      b. Singleness produces unique pressures (v. 28)
      c. Singleness offers special freedom (v. 32)
      d. Singleness bestows unusual opportunities (vv. 32–35)

II. Singleness and the society
  A. The secular society
    1. Projecting an image of freedom and fulfillment
      a. No commitments
      b. No ties
      c. No restraints
    2. Providing opportunities that deny the image
      a. Companionship but no commitment
      b. "Meaningful experiences" without ties
      c. Fulfillment without significance
    3. Producing a group of disappointed and hurting people
  B. The church society
    1. Not always sympathetic to the single
    2. Sometimes suspicious of the single
    3. Occasionally insensitive to singleness

III. Singleness and the single
  A. Evaluating the singleness calling

     1. Seeing the divine perspective (see I.B.3.a. above)
     2. Seizing the God-given opportunity
  B. Identifying the causes of singleness
     1. Single by choice
       a. Shyness
       b. Fear
       c. Immaturity
       d. Conviction
     2. Single by chance
       a. Widowed
       b. Divorced
       c. Deserted
       d. Lack of opportunity
  C. Countering the consequences of singleness
     1. Loneliness countered by service
     2. Bitterness countered by forgiveness
     3. Sensuality countered by obedience
     4. Worthlessness countered by involvement

16

What Do Real Teenagers Do?

Luke 2:41-52

Adolescence–the period of growth from puberty to maturity–is a twentieth-century word that is not an exclusively twentieth-century experience. But some people feel that this stage through which we all pass is particularly difficult in the modern world. What does a real teenager do about it?

I. Teenager, consider yourself
    A. You are a person in process (v. 52)
        1. Psychological growth–"wisdom" (James 3:13–18)
            a. Accumulation of information
            b. Application to situation
            c. Attitude leading to motivation
            d. Actions producing mobilization
        2. Physiological growth–"stature" (John 9:21–23)
            a. Stature changes

   b. Sexual changes
   c. Skin changes
3. Spiritual growth—"favor with God"
   a. A faith born of conformity
   b. A faith battered by challenge
   c. A faith built on conviction
4. Social growth—"favor with man"
   a. The social structures of parents
      (1) Values
      (2) Controls
      (3) Provisions
      (4) Security
B. The social attractions of peers
   1. Excitement
   2. Experiment
   3. Acceptance
C. The social challenges of the opposite sex
   1. Attraction
   2. Discovery
D. You are a person under pressure
   1. Psychological pressure
      a. Knowing how to behave
      b. Discovering what is acceptable
   2. Physiological pressure
      a. Handling sexual urges
      b. Evaluating sexual mores
      c. Understanding physical symptoms
   3. Spiritual pressure
      a. The beginnings of doubt
      b. The implications of belief
   4. Social pressure
      a. The desire for independence
      b. The need for assurance
E. You are a person with potential (Eccles. 12:1–7)
   1. The bowl on the cord

    2. The pitcher at the spring
    3. The wheel by the well

II. Teenager, control yourself
  A. Avoid developing unhealthy attitudes
  B. Avoid engaging in illegitimate activities
  C. Avoid drifting into spiritual apathy
  D. Avoid embracing unhelpful alliances

III. Teenager, concern yourself
  A. With the development of your personality
  B. With your physical well-being
  C. With the establishment of spiritual values
  D. With the nurturing of lasting relationships

17

Do Real Parents Ever Succeed?

Deuteronomy 6:1–25; Ephesians 6:1–4

This question is being asked today because many parents suspect they may have failed and many children do little to alter the perception. But to answer the question we need to know what parents are supposed to do.

I. Parents succeeding as people
  A. People of principle (Deut. 6:1–25)
      1. Listening to the Lord your God (vv. 1–3)
      2. Obeying the Lord your God (v. 3)
      3. Loving the Lord your God (v. 5)
      4. Honoring the Lord your God (v. 13)
      5. Serving the Lord your God (v. 13)
      6. Trusting the Lord your God (vv. 18–19)
  B. People of practicality
      1. Translating principles into relationships
          a. Partner relationships
          b. Progeny relationships

      2. Translating principles into righteousness (v. 25)
         a. Living rightly before God
         b. Treating God's people rightly

II. Parents succeeding as providers (1 Tim. 5:8; 2 Cor. 12:14)
    A. Providing protection
      1. Keeping them healthy
      2. Keeping them happy
      3. Keeping them human
    B. Providing direction
      1. Moral and spiritual direction (Deut. 6:6–8)
         a. Teaching by explanation
         b. Teaching by example
      2. Practical and societal direction (Prov. 22:6)
         a. Discovering the way he should go
         b. Assisting him to get there
    C. Providing inspection (Prov. 29:15)
      1. Don't leave a child to himself
      2. Don't invade a child's privacy
    D. Providing correction (Prov. 22:15; 2 Tim. 3:16)
      1. The discipline that disciples
      2. The discipline that destroys

III. Parents succeeding at perfection!
    A. Beware unrealistic expectations
      1. Children have minds of their own (Isa. 1:2)
      2. Parents can only give them the material
    B. Beware excessive pressure (Eph. 6:4; Col. 3:21)
      1. Unfair demands
      2. Unfulfilled promises
      3. Inconsistent behavior
      4. Uninvolved lifestyle

C. Beware ignoring failure
   1. Come to grips
   2. Admit the truth
   3. Seek forgiveness
   4. Restore the lost opportunities
D. Beware discounting God
   1. The power of intercession
   2. The possibility of intervention

18

Are Real Workers Cursed or Called?

Ecclesiastes 2:1-26

As we spend half our conscious hours at work—give or take a few hours—our attitudes toward work form a significant part of our attitude toward life. How are we to view work? Is it a curse or a calling?

I. Common attitudes toward work
   A. Wendell Workaholic—life is work
   B. Lenny Lazy—here am I, send him
   C. Pavlov Paycheck—work is money
   D. Randy Ripoff—if it's there, it's there to be taken
   E. Fanny Frazzle—not enough hours in the day
   F. Buck Bossman—workers of the world unite
   G. Cuthbert Coronary—life is bills and taxes
   H. Percy Plodder—a day's work for a day's pay
   I. Cindy Cheerleader—this is the finest, biggest, bestest institution east of the Mississippi

Results:
1. Worker dissatisfaction
2. Plummeting productivity
3. Management misery

II. Christian approaches to work
  A. Work from a Scriptural perspective
    1. The creative work of the Father (Gen. 1)
    2. The mandated work of mankind (Gen. 2)
    3. The tarnished work of the fall (Gen. 3)
    4. The abused work of the captives (Exod. 1)
    5. The finished work of the Savior
  B. Work from a self-fulfillment perspective
    1. God-likeness is part of our uniqueness
    2. Creativity is part of our humanness
    3. Giftedness is part of our glory
    4. Completeness is related to productiveness
  C. Work from a societal perspective
    1. The Savior's example of service (John 13:1–17)
    2. The Lord's call to serve (Matt. 5:14–16)
  D. Work from a spiritual perspective
    "Orare est laborare; laborare est orare"
    1. The "calling" aspect (1 Cor. 7:20; Col. 3:17)
    2. The "cooperating" aspect (Gen. 2:15; 2 Cor. 6:1)
    3. The "caring" aspect (Eph. 4:28; 2 Tim. 2:6; 1 Tim. 5:8)
    4. The "offering" aspect (2 Cor. 8; 9)

III. Corrective adjustments to work
  A. Management adjustments
    1. The master has his master (Col. 4:1)
  B. Employment adjustments
    1. Choice of employment
    2. Change of employment
    3. Challenge of employment

C. Unemployment adjustments
   1. Unemployed by chance
   2. Unemployed by choice
D. Retirement adjustments
   1. The possibilities of retirement
   2. The problems of retirement

19

Are Real Friends Necessities or Luxuries?

John 15:1-17

A recent survey found that "70 percent of Americans recognize that while they have many acquaintances, they have few close friends, and they experience this as a serious void in their lives."

I. The place of friendship
   A. Divine-human friendship
      1. God and Abraham (Isa. 41:8)
      2. God and Moses (Exod. 33:11)
      3. Jesus and disciples (John 15:1–17; 11:11; cf. James 4:4)
   B. Human friendship
      1. The friendship of man and woman
         a. In marriage (Prov. 2:17)
         b. Outside marriage (John 4:27)
      2. The friendship of woman and woman
         For example, "Thank you for being a friend"

    3. The friendship of man and man
        a. David and Jonathan (1 Sam. 18:1–4)
        b. Difficulties in modern culture
    4. The friendship of youth and age
        a. Barnabas and John Mark (Acts 15:37–38)
    5. The friendship of youth and youth
        a. Problematic peer pressure
        b. Positive peer pressure

II. The prize of friendship
    A. The longing for belonging (Prov. 17:17; 18:24)
    B. The consequences of cooperating (Eccles. 4:9–12)
    C. The possibilities of growing (Prov. 27:6–10)
    D. The privileges of sharing (Prov. 14:20–21)

III. The price of friendship
    A. Making friends
        1. Dimensions—acquaintance, tentative friendship, bosom buddies
        2. Dangers—bad choices (Prov. 6:1–5; 22:24–25)
        3. Demands—reciprocity, honesty, loyalty
    B. Maintaining friendships
        1. Caution (Prov. 12:26)
            a. Overkill (Prov. 25:17)
            b. Timing (Prov. 27:14)
            c. Insensitivity (Prov. 25:20); (also: Job's friends)
            d. Insincerity (Prov. 26:18–19)
        2. Commitment (3 John 14)
            a. To individual
            b. To group

3. Constancy
    a. Despite circumstances (Prov. 19:4–7; 27:10)
    b. Despite consequences (Matt. 26:50–56)
4. Candor
    a. The right kind (Prov. 28:23; 27:6; Eph. 4:15)
    b. The wrong kind (Prov. 16:28; 17:9; 29:5)

20

Do Real Christians Act Differently?

1 Corinthians 6:1-11

Chuck Colson summarized the findings of a number of observers when he said, "Religion is up, morality down." This may suggest that the moral impact of Christians on society is inadequate because the moral consequences of belief are not being seriously addressed by Christians.

I. The connection between behavior and belief
   A. The fundamentals of Christian belief
      1. The kingdom of God
         a. To be entered
         b. To be inherited
      2. The person of Christ
         a. His saviorhood
         b. His lordship
      3. The ministry of the Spirit
         a. In conviction
         b. In conversion

B. The fundamentals of Christian experience
  1. The experience of being washed
     a. The recognition of moral wickedness
     b. The purifying from moral guilt
  2. The experience of being justified
     a. The action of God in justification
     b. The acceptance by man of justification
  3. The experience of being sanctified
     a. The status of the sanctified
     b. The process of sanctification
C. The fundamentals of Christian behavior
  1. Behavior related to conversion
     a. What we were
     b. What we became
  2. Behavior related to separation
     a. The significance of association

II. The confusion of behavior and belief
  A. The confusion of mistaken belief
     1. That the immoral inherit the kingdom
     2. That the redeemed continue in immorality
  B. The confusion of false profession
     1. Those who call themselves brothers
     2. Those who contradict their profession

III. The confirmation of belief by behavior
  A. The desire for newness of life
  B. The dynamics of newness of life
  C. The decisions of newness of life

21

Do Real Disciples Pursue Trivia?

Mark 8:27-38

Trivial Pursuit may be more than the name of a popular game. It may describe some contemporary attitudes toward life. Someone has suggested that modern men have "the inalienable right to life, liberty and the pursuit of trivia." But what do Christ's disciples do?

I. Disciples confront Christ's issues
   A. The issue of life's possibilities (vv. 35–37)
      1. The possibility of a wasted life
      2. The possibility of a worthwhile life
   B. The issue of life's problems
      1. The problem of satanic influence (v. 33)
      2. The problem of secular mind-set (v. 33)
      3. The problem of societal corruption (v. 38)

II. Disciples confirm Christ's claims
   A. He is the real Christ (v. 28)
      1. Mistaken ideas
      2. False messiahs

B. He is the rejected Christ (v. 31)
   1. By political elders
   2. By religious priests
   3. By moral teachers
C. He is the redemptive Christ (v. 31)
   1. Healing society's hurts
   2. Dealing with society's sin
D. He is the risen Christ (v. 31)
   1. Not a victim
   2. But a victor
E. He is the reigning Christ (v. 38)
   1. The final authority
   2. The ultimate judge

III. Disciples consent to Christ's will
   A. They choose to come after him (v. 34)
      1. Like a learner
      2. Like a lover
      3. Like a servant
   B. They choose to deny themselves (v. 34)
      1. The initial decision
      2. The continual struggle
   C. They choose to take up their cross (v. 34)
      1. The path the Master trod
      2. The servant is not greater than the Master
   D. They choose to follow Christ
      1. Not to be ashamed (v. 38)
      2. Not to be delivered

Part 3

What's the Difference?

22

What Does "Born Again" Mean?

John 3:1-21

Ever since Jimmy Carter announced that he was running for president and that he had been "born again," the term has been in vogue. It has also been misused, abused, and generally depreciated. The question we need to ask is, Is the new birth an important aspect of spiritual experience?

I. The new birth is absolutely essential
   A. You must be born again (v. 7)
   B. Without it the kingdom of God is unattainable (v. 5)
   C. Without it the kingdom of God is not understandable (v. 3)
   D. Verily, verily!

II. The new birth is of God not man
   A. Water and the Spirit (v. 5)
      1. Water equals cleansing?

       2. Water equals procreation?
       3. Water equals baptism?
    B. Flesh produces flesh; spirit produces spirit (v. 6)
       1. Nicodemus the Pharisee
       2. Nicodemus the wistful (v. 4)
    C. Earthly produces earthly; heavenly, heavenly
       (vv. 12–13)
       1. Nicodemus the teacher
       2. Jesus came from heaven

III. The new birth is mysterious and wonderful (v. 8)
    A. When does it actually take place?
       1. Nicodemus the inquirer (vv. 1–2)
       2. Nicodemus the tentative (7:50–51)
       3. Nicodemus the disciple (19:39)
    B. How does it work?
       1. The inner working of the Spirit
          a. Revealing the condition of the heart
          b. Revealing the wonder of the cross
             (v. 14)
          c. Revealing the magnitude of the issues
             (v. 16)
       2. The inner response of the heart
          a. Believing in him (v. 16)
          b. Submitting to the kingdom (vv. 3, 5)

IV. The new birth is life changing (see Titus 3:5;
    1 Peter 1:23)

23

What Does It Mean to Be a Christian?

Acts 11:19-26

The name *Christian* was given to some of Christ's disciples as an uncomplimentary nickname, but in time it became a recognized designation for those who followed Christ. In more recent times the meaning of the term has become confused. A look at its origins should help.

I. To be a Christian means to be related to Christ
   A. Christian as a nominal concept
   B. Christian as a national concept
   C. Christian as a vital relationship
      1. The Lord Jesus was proclaimed (v. 20)
         a. The good news of Jesus
         b. The good news of Lord
      2. The Lord's hand was upon them (v. 21)
      3. The Lord was acknowledged (v. 21)
         a. Acknowledged by belief
         b. Acknowledged by turning to him

71

      c. Acknowledged by wholeheartedness (v. 23)
      d. Acknowledged by faithfulness

II. To be a Christian involves living faith
    A. Faith life that is stronger than persecution (v. 19)
    B. Faith life that desires to share the blessing (vv. 20, 29)
    C. Faith life that demonstrates grace in action (v. 23)
    D. Faith life that requires the power of the Spirit (v. 24)
    E. Faith life that is nourished in teaching (v. 26)
    F. Faith life that exhibits true discipleship

III. To be a Christian means to be a disciple of Jesus Christ (v. 27)
    A. Persuaded to be the point of commitment (Acts 26:28)
    B. Privileged to bear the name of Christ (1 Peter 4:16)
    C. Persevering to the end of the road

24

What Does It Mean to Be a Disciple?

Luke 5:1-11

Disciple" is not a commonly used word in ordinary conversations, but it should be a highly respected word in Christian thought because, among other things, our Lord's final instructions included the command to make disciples. What did he mean?

I. Willing to be challenged
A. The challenge of the call
1. The nature of the call
a. Invitation
b. Command
2. The process of the call (see John 1:40–42; Matt. 4:18–22; Luke 5:1–11)
a. Attention–Behold!
b. Attraction–We have found!
c. Authority–Follow me!
3. The purpose of the call
a. The Master-disciple relationship

B. The challenge of the consequences
1. Affections
   a. They left their father (Mark 1:20)
2. Allegiances
   a. Because you say so (Luke 5:5)
3. Acquisitions
   a. They left everything and followed him
   (v. 11)

II. Willing to be changed
A. By the One who knows it all (John 1:42)
1. "You are . . . You will be"
B. By the One who does it all (Luke 5:6–9)
1. Depart from me
C. By the One who doesn't give up
1. Simon Peter in the garden (Mark 14:31–42)
2. Simon Peter in the courtyard (Mark 14:53–72)
3. Simon Peter on the lake shore (John 21:1–19)
4. Simon Peter on the roof top (Acts 10:9–23)
5. Simon Peter in the dining room (Gal. 2:11–13)

III. Willing to be channeled
A. Channeled into his plan
"I will make you" (Mark 1:17)
B. Channeled into his priorities
"Men . . . not fish"
C. Channeled into his process
It takes time to make a fisherman

25

What Do We Mean by Forgiveness?

Matthew 18:21-35

Apparently Peter was frustrated when he asked Jesus, "Lord, how many times shall I forgive my brother?" Forgiveness is an integral part of Christian experience, so Peter was right to ask for help. Many of us need help with forgiveness, too.

I. The demands of forgiveness
   A. The demands of Christ's teaching (Luke 17:1–10)
      1. Relationships are full of difficulties
      2. Responsibility for action must be accepted
      3. Reactions must be carefully watched—they may be sinful
      4. Responses include rebuking and forgiving
         Note: the place of faith (vv. 5–6) and duty (vv. 7–10)

B. The demands of Christ's example (Luke 7:36–50)
1. Concern about people's brokenness
2. Compassion for people's helplessness
3. Commitment to people's wholeness
C. The demands of Christ's analogy (Matt. 18:21–35)
1. The linkage of being forgiven and being forgiving
   a. To receive but not give is immoral
   b. To request but deny is impossible (see Matt. 6:12)
2. The logic of being forgiven and being forgiving
   a. The immensity of man's debt to God
   b. The wonder of God's grace to man
   c. The relative magnitude of man's debt to man
   d. The necessity of man's forgiveness of his fellow

II. The difficulties of forgiveness
A. The difficulty of experiencing forgiveness (see Ps. 32:1–5)
1. Recognition of unhappiness
2. Reluctance to identify cause
3. Refusal to acknowledge sin
   Note how all this is changed
B. The difficulty of offering forgiveness
1. Inadequate understanding of divine forgiveness
2. Inappropriate handling of personal trauma
   a. Holding the other person responsible
   b. Making them pay
   c. Getting even

    C. The difficulty of applying forgiveness
       1. When the offender is unrepentant and unreceptive
       2. When we confuse forgiving and forgetting

III. The delights of forgiveness
    A. The delight of being a blessing
       1. Setting someone free to live again
       2. Letting someone know they're loved again
    B. The delight of being blessed
       1. The spiritual gift
       2. The emotional release
       3. The physical renewal

26

What Do We Mean by Mission?

John 17:12-18

Emil Brunner said, "The Church exists by mission as fire exists by burning." The evangelical church needs to be particularly aware of the nature, the necessity, and the nurture of mission if it is to avoid degenerating into a heap of ashes.

I. The necessity of the church's mission
   Note: Mission (Lat. *missio,* "a sending")–being sent out with authority to perform a special duty
   A. The character of God
      1. He sent his spokesmen, the prophets
      2. He sent his Son, the Savior (Gal. 4:4)
      3. He sent his Spirit, the Comforter (John 14:26)
      4. He sent his servants, the disciples (John 17:18)
      5. He sent the Scriptures, the Word (Isa. 55:11)
   B. The call of Christ
      1. The call to obtain comfort (Matt. 11:28–30)
      2. The call to obey commands (John 13:34)

3. The call to observe commissioning (Matt. 28:19–20)
C. The constitution of the church
   1. Constituted to be pervasive as leaven (Matt. 13:33)
   2. Constituted to be preservative as salt (Matt. 5:13)
   3. Constituted to be penetrative as light (Matt. 5:14)

II. The nature of the church's mission
A. Mission was modeled in Christ's ministry
   1. He announced a unique kingdom
   2. He purchased a universal freedom
   3. He evidenced an unusual compassion
   4. He presented an unequivocal challenge
B. Mission is mandated by man's makeup
   1. Man is not a soul-less body
   2. Man is not a body-less soul
   3. Man is not a soul-body in isolation
C. Mission was mapped out in Christ's mandate
   1. To teach what he commanded
   2. To continue all he started
   3. To facilitate what he desires

III. The nurturing of the church's mission
A. Nurturing through correctives
   1. Correcting selfish attitudes
   2. Correcting erroneous impressions
   3. Correcting unbalanced positions
B. Nurturing through directives
   1. Directing toward theology of mission
   2. Directing toward history of mission
   3. Directing toward opportunity of mission
C. Nurturing through initiatives
   1. Initiating a mission vision
   2. Initiating a mission experience
   3. Initiating a mission commitment

27

What Do We Mean by Eternal Security?

John 10:27-30; Hebrews 6:4-6

Eternal security is not a biblical term, neither is "once saved always saved," but both are used quite commonly among Christians. They relate to the question of whether Christians will always remain true to the Lord as long as they live or whether some may fall away.

I. The assurance factor
   A. Some biblical statements
      1. Our inheritance is guarded by God's power (1 Peter 3–5)
      2. Nothing can shake us free from God's love (Rom. 8:31–39)
      3. God will complete what he started (Phil. 1:6)
      4. Christ continues to intercede for his people (Heb. 7:25)
      5. God faithfully provides grace for all eventualities (1 Cor. 10:13)
      6. Christ's promises cannot fail (John 10:27–30)

B. Some theological inferences
Calvinism's TULIP
1. Total depravity
2. Unconditional predestination
3. Limited atonement
4. Irresistible grace
5. Perseverance
C. Some logical conclusions
1. Positive conclusions
   a. God's sovereignty presides over all
   b. God's grace is sufficient
   c. God's people are secure in him
2. Negative conclusions
   a. What about human choice and responsibility?
   b. The possibility of lax behavior
   c. The possibility of laziness in service

II. The warning factor
A. Some biblical statements
1. Christ warned about being led astray (Matt. 24:3–14)
2. Christians are to continue in the faith (Col. 1:21–23)
3. Those who stand may fall (1 Cor. 10:12)
4. The danger of drifting away from the truth (Heb. 2:1; 3:12–14)
5. The possibility of committing apostasy (Heb. 6:4–6)
6. Some examples: Saul, Judas, Demas, Ananias and Sapphira, Hymenaeus and Alexander
B. Some theological inferences
Arminianism's position
1. God is not willing that any should perish
2. The appeal to believe presupposes human ability

    3. If humans can believe, they can stop
      believing
  C. Some logical conclusions
    1. Positive conclusions
      a. Emphasizes human responsibility
      b. Stimulates to diligent living
      c. Encourages active service
    2. Negative conclusions
      a. Produces uncertainty
      b. Limits sovereignty

III. The practical factors
  A. The balance factor
    1. Divine sovereignty
    2. Human responsibility
  B. The burden factor
    1. Those who respond and disappear
    2. Those who believe but don't behave
  C. The behavior factor
    1. The careless and the indifferent
    2. The paranoid and the afraid

28

What about Divorce?

Matthew 19:1-12

It is often said that "marriages are made in heaven," but it must be admitted that many are lived elsewhere. The modern solution to marital difficulty is either to bypass marriage entirely or to get a divorce. But is this the way to go?

I. The issue Christ confronted
   A. A personal challenge
   B. A moral/spiritual/societal issue
      1. Qumran community—divorce illicit always
      2. Hillel school—divorce illicit always
      3. Shammai school—divorce permitted for "gross indecency" (see Deut. 24:1-4)
      4. Josephus—divorce permitted "for any cause whatsoever"

II. The response Christ gave
   A. A statement of divine intention

      1. Maleness and femaleness divinely ordained
      2. Public structure—"leave father and mother"
      3. Personal covenant—"united to his wife"
      4. Intimacy of commitment—"two become one flesh"
      5. Permanence of relationship—"God has joined . . . not separate"
  B. A rebuttal of Pharisaic teaching
      1. Why did Moses command? (Matt. 19:7)
      2. He didn't—he permitted (v. 8)
      3. Because of "hardness of heart"
      4. Divorce is not a human right
      5. It is, at best, a reluctant divine concession (see Mal. 2:13–16)
  C. A clarification of divine principle
      1. It is necessary to get back to "the beginning"
      2. Divorce for "every reason" not permissible
      3. Exception made for *porneia* (Gk.)
      4. Old Testament death penalty abolished
      5. Where divorce is permissible, remarriage is possible

III. The legacy Christ left
    What is the church to do about divorce?
  A. Uphold the institution of marriage
  B. Oppose the abuse of divorce
  C. Identify the causes of breakdown (see Matt. 15:19–20)
  D. Deal with "hardness of heart"
  E. Bring hope to the wounded (e.g., 1 Cor. 7:15)
  F. Show compassion to the wayward

29

What about Homosexuality?

Romans 1:18-32

D r. Gary Collins says, "There probably is no other word [homosexuality] in the English language which is so symbolic of controversy and which so quickly triggers emotional reactions." Our task is to think biblically about the subject and deal in a Christian manner with those who are involved.

I. Biblical statements about homosexuality
   A. Human sexuality
      1. A divine creation (Gen. 1:27; 2:18–23)
         a. Image of God—male and female
         b. Man—male and female
         c. Woman—answer to man's aloneness
      2. A divine gift
         a. Procreation—fruitful and multiply (Gen. 1:28)
         b. Celebration (e.g., Song of Solomon)
         c. Integration—one flesh

B. Homosexuality
1. Sodom and Gomorrah–gang rape (Gen. 19; Jude 7)
a. Note: "know" (Gen. 19:5, 8)
2. Holiness code (Lev. 18:22; 20:13)
a. Note: You must not do; you must obey (Lev. 18:3)
b. Homosexuality one of numerous prohibitions
3. Gibeah (Judges 19)
4. Gospels–silence on subject
a. Not a major problem in Israel
b. Jesus always assumes heterosexuality
5. Paul's teaching
a. Romans 1:26–27
(1) God's revelation resisted
(2) God's judgment revealed–"gave them up"
(3) Unnatural replaces natural– "inversion," "perversion"
b. 1 Corinthians 6:9; 1 Timothy 1:10
(1) Unrighteousness and lawlessness includes homosexual acts
(2) This leads to exclusion from kingdom

II. Contemporary attitudes about homosexuality
A. Definition
1. Attraction
2. Action
B. Condition
1. Constitutional
2. Learned behavior
C. Reaction
1. Homophobia
2. Acceptance and militant propagation
3. Rejection and concern

III. Christian responses to homosexuality
   A. Recognition of divine condemnation
   B. Sensitivity to human condition
   C. Commitment to compassionate ministry
   D. Conviction of spiritual possibilities (see 1 Cor. 6:10)

30

What about Shaky Marriages?

1 Corinthians 13:1-13

Marriages become shaky for a number of reasons, and there are numerous helpful ways of handling the problems. But there is one ingredient that all marriages need—*agapē* love. What it is and how it is experienced should top every marital agenda.

I. Dimensions of marital love
   A. Physical and sexual attraction and fulfillment—*Eros*
   B. Friendship and companionship—*Philia*
   C. Commitment to the other's well-being—*Agapē*
      1. A matter of duty (1 Cor. 14:1)
      2. A ministry of the Spirit (Gal. 5:22)

II. Descriptions of marital love (1 Cor. 13: 4–8)
    Note: love is more than a feeling—it behaves!
    A. Love suffers long—*makrothumia* (Gk.)

      1. Purpose
      2. Limits
   B. Love is kind
      1. Generosity of spirit
      2. Leads to repentance (Rom. 2:4)
   C. Love is not jealous
      1. Valid jealousy
      2. The possessiveness power
   D. Love is not boastful
      1. Insecurity's language
      2. Desire for approval at other's expense
   E. Love is not proud
      1. The essence of "me-ism"
      2. Deifying of self
   F. Love is not rude
      1. Rudeness despises, denigrates, and destroys
   G. Love is not self-seeking
      1. Self-seeking never serves
      2. It says me, not us; mine not ours
   H. Love is not irritable
      1. Instead of the personal hurt . . .
      2. The attempt to understand
   I. Love does not keep records
      1. Remembering
      2. Rehearsing
      3. Resenting
      4. Revenging
   J. Love does not enjoy evil
      1. Imagining it
      2. Assuming it
      3. Looking for it
   K. Love rejoices in truth
      1. Promoting it
      2. Protecting it
   L. Love always . . .
      1. Protects
      2. Trusts

        3. Hopes
        4. Perseveres
    M. Love does not fail
        1. Commitment
        2. Continuance

III. Dynamics of marital love
    A. Desire–to love
    B. Decision–to love
    C. Dedication–to go on loving
    D. Devotion–to source of love

31

What Exactly Is Materialism?

Matthew 6:19-34

Ivan Boesky told the graduating class at the University of California, Berkeley, "I think greed is healthy. You can be greedy and still feel good about yourself." Not many people would openly agree with him, but we all have to struggle with our attitudes toward material things.

I. What is materialism?
   A. Ancient views that material is evil
      1. Asceticism
      2. Epicureanism
      3. Contradicted by creation and incarnation
   B. Contemporary views that material is everything
      1. Communism
      2. Capitalism—in many forms
      3. Contradicted by Christ (Luke 12:15)
   C. Common view that material is somewhere in between

    1. A matter of "storing" (Matt. 6:19)
    2. A matter of "seeing" (v. 22)
    3. A matter of "serving" (v. 24)
    4. A matter of "seeking" (v. 32)

II. What is wrong with materialism?
    A. It stores the wrong things
        1. Treasures on earth, instead of . . .
        2. Treasures in heaven
            a. 1 Corinthians 13:13
            b. 1 Peter 3:4
            c. Colossians 3:23
            d. Luke 16:9
    B. It sees life through the wrong lens
    C. It serves the wrong master
        1. Either your materials are your god . . .
        2. Or your God is God of your materials
    D. It seeks the wrong satisfactions
        1. Eating, drinking, wearing, instead of . . .
        2. Kingdom and righteousness

III. What should we do about materialism?
    A. Recognize it—eyes full of light
    B. Reject it—who will be master?
    C. Resist it—an ongoing necessity
        1. By trusting in him, not what he made
        2. By seeing yourself as his, not yours
        3. By handling resources as a steward, not an owner

32

What Is the Sanctity of Life?

Genesis 1:26–28

In recent years there has been a tendency to talk about the "quality of life" rather than the "sanctity of life." Without in any way suggesting that the quality of life is without importance, we need to understand the change of emphasis and where it might lead.

I. The importance of the "sanctity of life" position
   A. Man is created in the divine image (Gen. 1:26–28)
      1. Intelligence—planning, executing, evaluating—"Let there be"
      2. Creativity—imagination, production—"It was so . . . very good"
      3. Leadership—develop, direct— "Have dominion"
      4. Community—togetherness, related—"Let us"
   B. Man is capable of divine fellowship
      1. Ability to know God—mind

    2. Capacity to love God—emotion
    3. Capability to obey God—will
  C. Man is called to divine purpose
    1. To glorify God
    2. To enjoy him forever
       Summary: man's significance determined
       by reference to God

II. The impact of the "quality of life" position
  A. The introduction of secularization
    1. Theism—faith in a God of order leading to
       reverent scientific inquiry
    2. Deism—faith in an "absentee-landlord"
       God
    3. Secularism—faith in man, who has
       superseded God
  B. The causes of secularization
    1. Attraction—to attractive alternatives
    2. Reaction—to religious shortcomings
    3. Distraction—by selfish considerations
  C. The impact of secularization
    1. Man's view of God
      a. Does not exist—but pray to him
        occasionally
      b. Does exist—but don't pray to him
    2. Man's view of man
      a. A machine
      b. A naked ape
      c. A number
      d. A collection of tissues
        Summary: man's significance
        determined by society

III. The implications of the trend
  A. Awareness is mandatory
    1. Personally

  2. Societally
  3. Legislatively
 B. Conviction is necessary
  1. Opposing that which dehumanizes man
  2. Exposing that which honors man—theistic humanism
 C. Action is appropriate
  1. Abortion
  2. Pornography
  3. World famine
  4. Arms limitation
  5. Injustice
  6. Environment
  7. World economy
  8. Resource utilization

33

What about Pain and Suffering?

1 Peter 1:3-9

The German theologian Helmut Thielecke said, "Americans have an inadequate view of suffering." Whether or not he was right, there is no shortage of suffering in America. We need to ensure that our view of it is "adequate."

   I. The realities of pain and suffering
      A. The immensity
      B. The intensity (e.g., Job)
         "If we are one in body, mind, and spirit, we are one in suffering and health." (David McKenna)
         1. Physical
         2. Psychological
         3. Relational
         4. Spiritual

II. The reasons for pain and suffering
    "When suffering comes we ask, 'Why me? Why this? Why now?'"
    A. Physical factors
       1. The nervous system
       2. The aging process
    B. Human factors
       1. Man's independence of God
       2. Man's inhumanity to man
       3. Man's insensitivity to need
    C. Satanic factors
       1. Strategy: destroy faith at all costs
       2. Tactics: attack at the weakest point
    D. Divine factors
       1. The challenge of the skeptic
          a. If God is good he is not God
          b. If God is God he is not good
       2. The conviction of the believer
          a. God is all-loving
          b. God is all-powerful
          c. God is all-wise
             (1) He could have chosen not to create
             (2) He could have created men who were not free
             (3) He could have created free men who would not sin
             (4) He could have created free men who would sin
             (5) He chose (4) because
                 "It is the best of all possible ways to achieve the best of all possible worlds." (Norman Geisler)

III. The response to pain and suffering
    A. The response of trust and dependence
       1. Because God in Christ has suffered

    2. Because none of the alternatives offer hope
       (see Job 13:15; 19:25; 23:10)
B. The products of trust and dependence
    1. The development of character (Rom.
       5:3–5)
    2. The development of compassion (2 Cor.
       1:3–4)
    3. The development of composure (2 Cor.
       4:16–18)

Part 4

Christians Awake!

34

Rising to the Challenge

The World Congress on Evangelism, held in Lausanne, Switzerland, in 1974, was followed in 1989 by a second congress in Manila, Philippines. The theme was: "Calling the whole church to take the whole Gospel to the whole world."

I. The whole Gospel
   A. Gospel defined
      ". . . good news of God's salvation from the powers of evil, the establishment of His eternal Kingdom and His final victory over everything which defies His purpose." *(Manila Manifesto)*
      1. The condition of mankind
         a. Dignified because of divine image
         b. Corrupted because of sin's power
         c. Condemned because of God's holiness
      2. The uniqueness of Christ
         "He alone is the Incarnate Son, the Savior, the Lord and the Judge and He alone, with the Father and the Spirit, is worthy of the worship, faith and obedience of all people." *(Manila Manifesto)*

B. Gospel defended
1. Against false gospels—denying sin, judgment, and Christ
2. Against half gospels—minimizing sin, maximizing human effort
3. Against relativism—all religions, spiritualities equally valid
4. Against syncretism—combining Christ and other faiths
C. Gospel declared
1. The proclamation of Word
2. The incarnation of deed

II. The whole world
A. Population
1. Approaching 6 billion
2. Committed—40 million in 1900; 500 million today
3. Uncommitted—1.5 billion nominally Christian
4. Unevangelized—2 billion minimal exposure, reachable
5. Unreached—2 billion never heard gospel of Christ
B. Problems
1. Urbanization—in 1900–9 percent city dwellers; 2000–50 percent.
2. Secularization—making transcendent meaningless
3. Modernization—loss of transcendence, tradition, truth
4. Deprivation—poverty at 2.4 billion; oppression, 400 million
5. Persecution—limited access, martyrdom, imprisonment

III. The whole church
  A. Recognizing the whole church
  B. Motivating the whole church–to care and be credible
  C. Mobilizing the whole church
    1. To witness
    2. To worship
    3. To sacrifice

35

Caring Enough to Share

Ephesians 1:3-14

It is one thing to "call the whole church to take the whole Gospel to the whole world," but it is another matter entirely to motivate the church to do it. What does it take?

I. We need to be clear about objectives
   The objectives of evangelism are:
   A. To glorify God (1:6, 12; 2:4–5)
      1. By explaining his purpose and person
      2. By exalting his Son
   B. To build the church (2:11–18)
      1. The church—a company of redeemed
      2. The church—an alternative society
   C. To meet the human need (2:1–5)
      1. The human condition—real need
      2. The human experience—felt need
   D. To instruct the uninformed (4:17–19)
      1. Futile thinking needs truth
      2. Darkened understanding needs light

II. We need to be concerned about obligations
    A. The corporate obligation of the church
        1. To be the body (4:16)
        2. To be the bride (5:25)
        3. To be the building (2:21)
    B. The individual obligation of the Christian
        1. To say what he or she knows
        2. To show what he or she is
        3. To share what he or she has

III. We need to counter the objections
    A. Philosophical objections
        1. The church should put its house in order
           "Imperfection is no excuse for inaction"
        2. Everybody should be free to believe what
           they wish
           "Exactly—so let's make sure they are
           informed"
        3. Every culture is as good as the next one
           "Good—so let's tell people how good
           Christian culture is"
    B. Personal objections
        1. I don't know enough
        2. I'm afraid of reactions
        3. I don't think it's my job
        4. I don't want to get involved

36

Reaching a City for Christ

Acts 4:23–5:32

Jerusalem, the city over which Christ literally wept because of its antagonism to the message of the prophets and its rejection of the Christ, became the center of first-century evangelism. Opponents of the church admitted that the Christians had "filled Jerusalem with their teaching." To know how they did it will help us reach our city for Christ.

    I. Attitudes of the church in Jerusalem
       A. The "prayer" attitude (4:23–31)
          1. Their prayer was instinctive (vv. 23–24)
          2. Their prayer was submissive (v. 24)
          3. Their prayer was authoritative (v. 25)
          4. Their prayer was imaginative (v. 27)
          5. Their prayer was imperative (vv. 29–30)
          6. Their prayer was effective (v. 31)

B. The "share" attitude (4:32–37)
   1. The burden they shared
   2. The goals they shared (v. 32)
   3. The resources they shared (v. 33)
   4. The grace they shared (v. 33)
C. The "dare" attitude (5:1–32)
   1. They dared to confront issues (vv. 1–11)
   2. They dared to be controversial (vv. 12–16)
   3. They dared to defy authorities (vv. 17–28)
   4. They dared to obey God (v. 29)
   5. They dared to speak the truth (vv. 30–32)

II. Activities of the church in Jerusalem
   A. A ministry of proclamation
      1. Taking the initiative
      2. Teaching the truth
         a. About new life (v. 20)
         b. About Christ (vv. 30–31)
      3. Taking the consequences
         a. The fury of the opposition (v. 33)
         b. The faithfulness of the convinced (v. 14)
   B. A ministry of application
      1. Meeting physical needs (vv. 15–16)
      2. Healing emotional hurts (6:1)
      3. Bridging racial barriers (6:1)

III. Achievements of the church in Jerusalem
   A. They fulfilled their mandate from the Lord (Matt. 28)
   B. They filled their city with the gospel
   C. They furnished everyone an opportunity

37

Earning the Right to Be Heard

Acts 6:1–7:60

Stephen was the first Christian martyr. He was also a singularly effective witness to Christ. His secret was that he lived in the fullness of the Spirit, and this was evident to all who met him. This earned him the right to be heard.

I. What he was—irreproachable
   A. The believers knew what he was (6:3)
      1. Full of the Spirit and wisdom
      2. Full of faith and of the Holy Spirit (v. 5)
      3. Full of grace and power (v. 8)
   B. The opposition saw what he was
      1. Before the Sanhedrin (v. 15)
      2. Before the mob (7:59–60)

II. What he did—irrefutable
   A. What he did "among the people" (6:8)
      "Great wonders and marvelous signs"

    B. What he did when facing opposition
       Met the challenge with grace and dignity
    C. What he did when facing death
       1. Calmly entrusted his spirit to the Lord
         (7:59)
       2. Sought forgiveness for his murderers (7:60)

III. What he said—irresistible (6:10)
    A. The promise of the Savior (Luke 21:10–19)
    B. The power of the Spirit
    C. The pertinence of the Scriptures

38

How to Talk about God

"Witnessing," "sharing your faith," "spreading the gospel" mean different things to different people, but they all include talking about God. So let's talk about talking about God.

I. Why should we talk about God?
   A. Some say: "My faith is a personal matter"
      But God says: (Rom. 10:9; Ps. 107:2; Matt. 10:32)
   B. Some say: "It's the preacher's job"
      But God says: (Eph. 4:11–12; 2 Tim. 2:2)
   C. Some say: "People should be free to believe whatever they wish"
      But God says: (2 Tim. 3:16–17)
   D. Some say: "Actions speak louder than words"
      But God says: (Matt. 5:16; 12:34)

II. Why do we find it difficult to talk about God?
    Note: Moses' experience (Exod. 3:4–4:17)
    A. Lack of content
    B. Lack of courage

    C. Lack of concern
    D. Lack of confidence

III. How can we prepare to talk about God?
    A. Consecration (1 Peter 3:15)
        1. Spiritual preparation—"Christ as Lord"
        2. Mental preparation—"reasons for hope"
    B. Concern
        1. For God's glory (Eph. 1:13–14)
        2. For gospel's triumph (2 Thess. 3:1)
        3. For people's condition (1 Cor. 1:18)
    C. Contact
        1. Long term—building relationships
        2. Short term—recognizing opportunities
           Note: remember the eternal triangle
    D. Conversation
        1. Starting at the point of interest
        2. Leading to the point of the gospel
    E. Conclusion
        1. When to conclude
        2. How to conclude
    F. Continuation

39

Loving God and People

Romans 5:1-11; 2 Corinthians 5:14-21

One of the most dramatic conversions in the history of Christianity was that of Saul of Tarsus. From being the archenemy of Christ he became the great apostle. He explained that it was because "the Son of God . . . loved me and gave himself for me" (Gal. 2:20).

  I. The love of God explained (Rom. 5:1–11)
     A. The human condition
        1. Sinners (v. 8)
           a. A universal condition (3:23)
           b. An undeniable condition (fall short equals lack)
           c. An unacceptable condition (cf. good, righteous, 5:7)
        2. Powerless (v. 6)
           a. Incapable of living rightly
           b. Unable to rectify situation

      3. Ungodly (v. 6)
        a. Irreverence, impiety
        b. Attitudes toward God
      4. Enemies (v. 10)
        a. Active–human hostility Godward
        b. Passive–divine disapproval manward
  B. The divine action
      1. The motivation
        a. God's own love (v. 8)
        b. While we were still . . . (vv. 6, 8)
      2. The action
        a. Christ's death
        b. *Hyper* (Gk.) equals "on behalf of"
  C. The eternal consequences
      1. Justification experienced (v. 9)
      2. Salvation anticipated (v. 10)
      3. Reconciliation received (v. 11)

II. The love of God experienced
  For Saul–the Damascus Road
  A. The light shone on Christ
      1. He saw who he was
      2. He realized what he had done
  B. The light shone on Paul
      1. He saw who he was
      2. He realized what he had done
        Love conquers

III. The love of God expressed (2 Cor. 5:14–21)
  A. We are "hemmed" in by his love
  B. We no longer live for ourselves, but for him
  C. We regard no one from a worldly point of view
  D. We are ambassadors, agents of reconciliation

40

Reaching the Individual

"Whole church" and "whole world" concepts may obscure the importance of the individual. It is important to note that even in "the Acts," where the dramatic spread of the gospel is chronicled, great emphasis is placed on individuals coming to faith. We should be aware of how this generally happens.

   I. The seeking soul (Deut. 4:29; Isa. 55:6–7)
      A. The Ethiopian (Acts 8)
         1. Coming from a place of privilege, prestige, and power
         2. Seeking enough to travel (v. 27)
         3. Seeking enough to worship (v. 27)
         4. Seeking enough to study (v. 30)
         5. Seeking enough to inquire (v. 31)
      B. The Pharisee (Acts 9)
         1. Coming from a position of orthodoxy and zeal
         2. Kicking against the goads (26:14)
         3. Disturbed by Christian testimony (8:1)
         4. Blinded by revelation (Acts 9:12)

    C. The Roman (Acts 10)
        1. Coming from a background of state polytheism
        2. Open to evaluate pagan worship
        3. Ready to embrace monotheism
        4. Eager to lead a life of devotion (v. 2)
        5. Willing to follow divine promptings (vv. 7–8)

II. The gracious God (John 6:44; 2 Peter 3:9)
    A. Taking the initiative
        1. Scriptures (Acts 8:32)
        2. Spirit (Acts 7:51)
        3. Son (Acts 9:5)
    B. Recognizing the human condition (Acts 10:4)
    C. Reaching out to the seeker
        1. Sending help
        2. Using people

III. The willing worker
    A. Philip (Acts 8)
        1. Willing to be interrupted (v. 26)
        2. Willing to be directed (vaguely!)
        3. Willing to be direct (v. 30)
    B. Ananias (Acts 9)
        1. Willing to risk (vv. 13–14)
        2. Willing to trust (vv. 15–16)
        3. Willing to embrace (v. 17)
    C. Peter (Acts 10)
        1. Willing to deal with personal prejudice (v. 14)
        2. Willing to do the unconventional (v. 28)
        3. Willing to have his horizons broadened (vv. 34–35)

41

Grasping the Opportunities

Acts 11:19-30

Pogo said, "We are confronted with insurmountable opportunities"—a positive statement if ever there was one! The disciples of Christ demonstrated a similar attitude when they had to leave Jerusalem under intense pressure.

I. An opportunity to show their faith
   A. Faith undergoing . . .
      1. *Thlipsis* (Gk.)—"pressure, squeezing, crushing" (v. 19)
      2. *Diōgmos* (Gk.)—"hunting, pursuing" (8:1)
      3. *Peirasmos* (Gk.)—"testing" (cf. Luke 8:13; Matt. 13:21; Mark 4:17)
   B. Faith overcoming . . .
      1. By recognizing the inevitability (John 15:20; 2 Tim. 3:12)

    2. By rejoicing in the possibility (Rom. 5:3;
       8:35–39)
    3. By reflecting this certainty (Acts 9:16;
       2 Cor. 12:10)

II. An opportunity to share their faith
  A. The message—"the Lord Jesus" (Acts 11:20)
    1. The person of the Lord Jesus (10:38)
    2. The position of the Lord Jesus (10.36, 42)
    3. The peace of the Lord Jesus (10:36)
    4. The promise of the Lord Jesus (10:43)
    5. The power of the Lord Jesus (10:38)
  B. The method
    1. Speaking (Acts 11:19)
    2. Preaching (v. 20)
    3. Teaching (v. 26)
  C. The mystery
    1. The Lord's hand (v. 21)
    2. The people's response (v. 21)
      a. Believing
      b. Turning (cf. 26:18)
      c. Cleaving (Acts 11:23)

III. An opportunity to spread their faith
  A. Locally through consistent discipleship
  B. Socially through practical concern (vv. 28–30)
  C. Internationally through missionary
    involvement (13:1–3)

42

Sharing the Blessing

Acts 11:19-30; 13:1-3

The church at Antioch quickly became the major base of operations for worldwide evangelization. It is important that churches learn from their example.

I. Blessings received (11:19–30)
   A. The gospel received
      1. A great message
      2. A great response (vv. 21, 24, 26)
   B. The grace received (v. 23)
      1. The impact of grace
      2. The evidence of grace (Note: *Christianoi* Gk.)
   C. The gifts received (see Eph. 4:11–13)
      1. Gifted evangelists
      2. Gifted teachers
         a. Making disciples (11:26)
         b. Building church (v. 26)
         c. Encouraging believers (v. 23)

3. Gifted prophets
   a. Foretelling (v. 28)
   b. Forthtelling

II. Blessings acknowledged (13:1–3)
   A. Worshiping (v. 2)
   B. Fasting (v. 2)
   C. Listening
   D. Obeying (v. 3)
   E. Praying (v. 3)

III. Blessings Shared
   A. Because of a sense of concern (11:29–30)
   B. Because of a sense of calling (13:2)
   C. Because of a sense of commitment (13:3)
   D. Because of a sense of cooperation (14:26–28)

Part 5

Problem Areas

43

Understanding the Holy Spirit

Some believers are apprehensive of the Holy Spirit because they think he is some kind of ghost. Others have been frightened about him because they think he specializes in strange behavior. A little understanding goes a long way.

I. Who is the Holy Spirit?
- A. The mystery of the Trinity
- B. The mastery of the Father
- C. The majesty of the Son
- D. The ministry of the Spirit

II. What does the Holy Spirit do?
- A. S—He seals (Eph. 1:13)
  1. To hear
  2. To believe
  3. To mark as a possession (Eph. 4:30)
- B. P—He promotes (John 16:7–15)
  1. He promotes reality in life
  2. He promotes growth in knowledge
  3. He promotes experience of Christ

C. I–He indwells (Eph. 3:14–20)
   1. He is life in the place of deadness
   2. He is strength in the place of weakness
D. R–He resists (Gal. 5:16–21)
   1. The presence of the sinful nature
   2. The objective of the Holy Spirit
   3. The conflict between the two
E. I–He invests (1 Cor. 12:1–11)
   1. The *pneumatika* (Gk., v. 1) and *charismata* (Gk., v. 4)
   2. For the common good (v. 7)
   3. To be identified and utilized
F. T–He transforms (2 Cor. 3:16–18)
   1. The revelation of Christ
   2. The reflection of Christ
   3. The reproduction of Christ (Gal. 5:22–23)

III. What should we do?
   A. Attempt to be aware of him
   B. Bring the burden to him
   C. Choose to be controlled by him (Eph. 5:18)

44

What Is Involved in Church Life?

When Paul wrote to Timothy he wanted, among other things, to outline to him "how people ought to conduct themselves in God's household, which is the church of the living God" (1 Tim. 3:15). What he had to say is extremely relevant today.

I. Christian perception of the church (1 Timothy)
   A. The church is God's family (3:15)
      1. It enjoys his life
      2. It bears his name
      3. It projects his image
   B. The church is God's army
      1. It acknowledges his commands (1:1, 3, 5)
      2. It identifies with his cause
      3. It fights in his battles (1:18; 6:12)
   C. The church is God's academy
      1. The pillar and foundation of truth (3:15)
      2. The protector and preserver of truth (1:3; 6:3–5)
      3. The teacher and promoter of truth (4:11–16)

D. The church is God's community
1. The community of the redeemed (1:15)
2. The community of the reformed (1:16)
3. The community of the responsible (2:1–2)
4. The community of the respected (3:1–7)

II. Christian participation in the church (1 Timothy)
A. Participation in the family
1. The family roots
2. The family relationships (5:1–3)
3. The family realities
B. Participation in the army
1. The recognition of authority
2. The acceptance of discomfort
3. The conflict of involvement
C. Participation in the academy
1. Careful attention to learning
2. Continual attention to loving (1:5)
D. Participation in the community
1. Rights and responsibilities (5:3–4)
2. Service and selfishness (5:9–10)
3. Faithfulness and favoritism (5:21)

45

What Is Living by Faith?

When Paul said, "The life I live in the body, I live by faith in the Son of God" (Gal. 2:20), he outlined a basic principle of Christian experience that needs to be understood.

I. Faith as a principle
   A. The natural principle
      1. Creaturely dependence
      2. Creaturely interdependence
   B. The spiritual principle
      1. Faith as the principle of justification (Rom. 3:28)
         a. The impossibility of the alternatives
         b. The possibilities of the reality
      2. Faith as the principle of living
         a. We live by faith (Rom. 1:17)
         b. We walk by faith (2 Cor. 5:7)
         c. We stand by faith (2 Cor. 1:24)
         d. We pray by faith (James 5:15)
         e. We conquer by faith (1 John 5:4)

II. Faith as a practicality (see Rom. 4:17–25)
  A. Faith is confidence in a person
    1. The object of faith determines its validity
    2. The knowledge of the object determines its reality
  B. Faith is conversant with the problems
    1. Faith is not the evasion of problems
    2. Faith is the relating of problems
  C. Faith is consistent in its progress
    1. Faith is strengthened by adversity
    2. Faith thrives on faithfulness
  D. Faith is convinced of the promises
    1. Promises and integrity
    2. Promises and authority
    3. Promises and ability

III. Faith as a problem area
  A. The problem of divorcing faith from fact
    1. Trusting what isn't is!
    2. Trusting what won't be will!
  B. The problem of confusing faith and works
    1. Works are no substitute for faith
    2. Works are a valid evidence of faith
  C. The problem of preferring faith to obedience
    1. Trusting God to do what he didn't promise
    2. Trusting God to do what he commanded you to do
  D. The problem of ignoring faith all together
    1. The myth of self-sufficiency
    2. The reality of spiritual conflict

46

Handling Temptation

M odern man thinks of *temptation* as "seduction," but the term when used in the Bible means "to put a person to the test," whether benevolently to show his qualities or malevolently to expose his weaknesses. We need a biblical view of temptation.

I. Temptation needs to be understood
   A. Its origin
      1. God put his people to the test
         a. To reveal their true condition (Gen. 22:1–2)
         b. To purify their faith (1 Peter 1:6–7)
         c. To produce character (James 1:2–4)
         d. To assure them of his love (Rom. 5:3–11)
      2. Satan tempts God's people
         a. By crushing them (Job 1:11–22)
         b. By encouraging wrong satisfaction of valid desires
         c. By making them complacent and careless (Gal. 6:1)
         d. By misrepresenting God (Matt. 4:5–11)

B. Its potential
  1. Opportunity to go wrong or do right
  2. Opportunity for seduction or strengthening
  3. Opportunity to prove our weakness or project God's power
  4. Opportunity for devil to destroy or for God to develop

C. Its dimensions
  1. Temptation is never sin (Heb. 4:15)
  2. Temptation does not originate with God (James 1:13)
  3. Temptation is never too much to bear (1 Cor. 10:13)

II. Temptation needs to be handled
  A. The place of discernment
    1. Discernment of spiritual principles (Rom. 6:1–4)
      a. The principle of death to the old life
      b. The principle of aliveness to the new
    2. Discernment of personal weaknesses (James 1:14)
      a. Know what they are
      b. Know how to handle them
  B. The place of discretion
    1. Discretion about amount of exposure
    2. Discretion about need for assistance
  C. The place of decision
    1. Decision about spiritual position (Rom. 6:2)
    2. Decision about spiritual aspirations (Matt. 6:13)
    3. Decision about individual situations (Rom. 6:11–14)
      a. Reckoning
      b. Refusing
      c. Yielding not
      d. Yielding unto

47

Discipline and Obedience

M any values are under attack in our society, but at the root of the contemporary attitude is a resistance to the principle of obedience.

I. The meaning of obedience
   A. The etymological meaning
      1. Hebrew *šāmaᶜ* literally, "to hearken to" (1 Sam. 15:22)
      2. Greek
         a. *Hypakouō*–literally, "to hear under"
         b. *Eisakouō*–literally, "to hear into"
         c. *Peithōmai*–literally, "to yield to persuasion"
         d. *Peitharcheō*–literally, "to submit to authority"
   B. The theological meaning
      1. To accept God's authority
      2. To follow God's direction

II. The importance of obedience
A. Obedience as a creation principle (Gen. 2:15-17)
   1. The consciousness of authority
   2. The constitution of humanity
   3. The consequences of disobedience
B. Obedience as a salvation principle
   1. The obedience in the garden (Luke 22:42)
   2. The obedience unto death (Phil. 2:8)
C. Obedience as a faith principle
   1. The gospel requires the obedience of faith (Rom. 1:5)
   2. Faith is obedience to the divine order of salvation

III. The discipline of obedience
A. The discipline of recognizing the areas of obedience
   1. Obedience in spiritual life (Luke 6:46)
   2. Obedience in family life
      a. Obedient fathers (Heb. 11:8)
      b. Obedient mothers (1 Peter 3:6)
      c. Obedient children (1 Peter 1:14)
   3. Obedience in church life
      a. The character of the leaders (Titus 1:7-9)
      b. The attitude of the led (Heb. 13:17)
   4. Obedience in business life
      a. The obedience of masters (Eph. 6:9)
      b. The attitude of servants (Eph. 6:5-7)
   5. Obedience in civic life
      a. The charge to the authorities (Rom. 13:6)
      b. The responsibility of the governed (Titus 3:1)

B. The discipline of utilizing the aids to obedience
    1. The aids of the love life (John 14:15)
    2. The aids of the thought life (2 Cor. 10:5)
    3. The aids of the spirit life (Gal. 5:22–23)
    4. The aids of the communal life (Eph. 5:21)
C. The discipline of neutralizing the hindrances to obedience
    1. Neutralizing internal dynamics (Eph. 2:2)
    2. Neutralizing external factors (2 Tim. 3:1–2)

48

Discovering and Doing God's Will

There is a natural tendency for human beings to concentrate on themselves and to see everything as it relates to them. We need to learn, however, to start with God and see how everything relates to him. This includes an understanding of his will, what it is, and how we discover and do it.

I. Desiring God's will
  A. Recognizing God has a plan
    1. Consistent with his character (Eph. 1:5–19)
    2. Cosmic in its scope (1 Cor. 15:20–28)
  B. Believing God's plan is good (Rom. 12:1–2)
  C. Identifying the distinctives of God's plan
    1. The distinctive of spiritual maturity
       (1 Thess. 4:3)
    2. The distinctive of worshipful attitudes
       (1 Thess. 5:18)
    3. The distinctive of eternal assurance (John
       6:35–40)

   4. The distinctive of societal impact (1 Peter
      2:13–15)
   5. The distinctive of personal commitment
      (1 Peter 4:19)
   D. Desiring God's plan to be implemented
      1. The illustration of the Lord Jesus (Heb.
         10:7)
      2. The application of the Lord's example
         (1 Peter 4:1–2)

II. Discovering God's will
   A. Spiritual considerations
      1. The attitude of the believer (Rom. 12:1–2)
      2. The activity of the Spirit (1 Cor. 2:9–10)
      3. The application of the Scriptures
         (Ps. 37:4–5; Prov. 3:5–6)
         a. The place of condition
         b. The place of promise
   B. Practical considerations
      1. The green-light principle for everyday
         living
      2. The runway principle for crisis decisions
         a. Inner convictions
         b. External circumstances
         c. Concerned advice
         d. Scriptural affirmation
         e. Common sense

III. Doing God's Will
   A. Doing the will of God from the heart (Eph.
      6:6)
   B. Doing the will of God through the Spirit (Heb.
      13:21)
   C. Doing the will of God through cooperation
      (Phil. 2:12–13)

49

Money

One of the world's best known misquotations is "Money is the root of all evil." See 1 Timothy 6:10 for the real story! It is the attitude toward money that counts.

I. Attitudes toward money
   A. Money as master
      1. International conflicts
      2. Marital problems
      3. Crime involvement
      4. Moral corruption (1 Tim. 6:9; Luke 18:24)
   B. Money as means
      1. Usefulness as means of exchange
      2. Usefulness as means of storing wealth
      3. Usefulness as means of displaying heart (cf. Mark 12:41; Luke 12:13)

II. Attitudes toward acquiring money
   A. Attitudes toward wealth
      1. Communist attitude—wealth belongs to state

2. Capitalist attitude—wealth belongs to individual
3. Christian attitude—wealth belongs to the Lord (Ps. 24:1)

B. Attitudes toward work
1. Work is good (Gen. 1:28–31; Eph. 4:28)
2. Work is necessary (1 Tim. 5:8)
3. Work honors God
   a. Displays God-given skills
   b. Utilizes God-given time
   c. Channels God-given energy
   d. Produces God-given wealth
4. Work exposes evil
   a. Laziness is inexcusable (Prov. 18:9; 2 Thess. 3:6–15)
   b. Carelessness is unsatisfactory (1 Thess. 4:11)
5. Work creates wealth
   a. Wealth not an end in itself
   b. Work not solely to produce wealth
   c. Wealth and work related to meaning of humanity

III. Attitudes toward handling money
A. Handling money by spending it
   Note: the Micawber dictum on income and expenditure
1. Starting off a marriage
2. Determining suitable standard from position, and so forth
3. Adjusting to changing circumstances
4. Evaluating extremes of extravagance, parsimony
5. Living within means
6. Developing strategy

B. Handling money by saving it
   1. The extreme of imprudence
   2. The extreme of hoarding (see Matt. 6:19–20)
C. Handling money by sharing it (see 2 Cor. 8:12–15)
   1. The principle of sharing (Eph. 4:28)
   2. The principle of tithing
   3. The principle of proportionate giving
   4. The principle of taxing (Matt. 22:21)
   5. The principle of responsible giving
      a. Identify genuine need
      b. Invest in legitimate work
      c. Insist on responsible stewardship

50

Living with Unbelievers

Part of the tension of the Christian life comes from the necessity for Christians to live their lives in an environment that may not be Christian—among people who are not necessarily believers.

I. How believers look at unbelievers
   A. Realistic appraisal
      1. God created all people
      2. All people have fallen short of his standards
      3. All people need to be reconciled to God
      4. The only way is through grace and faith
      5. Those who choose not to believe are not reconciled
   B. Genuine appreciation
      1. In the chaos there is genuine creativity
      2. In the sinfulness there is genuine sincerity
      3. In the selfishness there is genuine sensitivity
      4. In the decadence there is genuine decency

C. Deep apprehension
  1. Apprehension about the unbelievers' philosophy
     a. The unbelieving atheist
     b. The unbelieving moralist
     c. The unbelieving humanist
  2. Apprehension about the unbelievers' society
     a. Based on false premises
     b. Heading for wrong conclusions
     c. Producing erroneous results
     d. Making inadequate promises
     e. Offering false hope
  3. Apprehension about the believers' destiny
     a. The reality of perishing as an ongoing experience
     b. The reality of perishing as a final destiny

II. How believers live with unbelievers
  A. Believers in an unbelieving society
    1. Recognizing the society is pluralistic
    2. Understanding morality cannot be legislated
    3. Undertaking to stand for righteousness and justice
  B. Believers in an unbelieving family
    1. The believers' high regard for family structures
    2. The believers' heavy responsibility for family members
    3. The believers' deep sensitivity for family misunderstanding
    4. The believers' strong commitment to family blessing

  C. Believers in an unbelieving marriage
    1. Unequal yoke is forbidden
    2. Unequal marriage can occur through conversion
    3. The onus is on the believer
    4. The objective is the blessing of spouse and children
  D. Believers in an unbelieving business
    1. Responsibility to authority
    2. The limits of authority
    3. The importance of integrity

III. How believers love unbelievers
  A. The believers' sense of privilege
    1. The privilege of being salt and light
    2. The privilege of bringing light and truth
  B. The believers' sense of purpose
    1. To bring glory to God on earth
    2. To bring blessing of God to mankind
  C. The believers' sense of power
    1. The decision to love
    2. The dynamics of love
    3. The decisiveness of love

51

Prayer

The emphasis placed on prayer in the Bible cannot be missed, but the practical experience of prayer in many believers' lives is far short of all that the Scriptures seem to expect. Some practical help is necessary.

I. What is prayer?
   Prayer is the talking part of the divine-human relationship
   A. The relationship of unity (Rom. 7:4)
   B. The relationship of authority (Col. 3:24)
   C. The relationship of familiarity (John 15:15)

II. Why should I pray?
   A. Because I want to (see above)
   B. Because I'm told to (Matt. 6:9)
   C. Because I need to

III. What should I pray?
   A. P–praise
   B. R–repentance
   C. A–asking
   D. Y–yourself

IV. When should I pray?
   A. Regularly (Dan. 6:10)
   B. Spontaneously (Neh. 2:4)
   C. Continually (1 Thess. 5:17)

V. What is involved in praying?
   A. Praying in Christ's name (John 14:13)
   B. Praying in God's will (1 John 5:14–15)
   C. Praying in the Spirit (Rom. 8:16, 26)
   D. Praying in faith (James 1:5–7)
   E. Praying with thanksgiving (Col. 4:2)

VI. What hinders prayer?
   A. Disobedience (1 John 3:22)
   B. Faulty marital relationships (1 Peter 3:6–7)
   C. Inappropriate attitude to sin (Ps. 66:18)
   D. Unsatisfactory motivation (James 4:1–3)

VII. What helps prayer?
   A. Attention to formal prayer
   B. Emulation of written prayers
   C. Discipline of personal prayer
      1. Time
      2. Place
      3. List
      4. Partner
   D. Sharing in corporate prayer

52

Personal Salvation

One of the most basic and important statements of Scripture is "For it is by grace you have been saved through faith" (Eph. 2:8). An understanding of this principle is imperative for personal well-being, church health, and viability of mission.

  I. The human condition
    A. We were dead (Eph. 2:1)
       1. The meaning of deadness
          a. The absence of life
          b. The alienation from God
       2. The causes of deadness
          a. Sins—failure to be
          b. Trespasses—actions that are forbidden
       3. The evidences of deadness
          Lack of
          a. Appetite
          b. Awareness
          c. Activity
    B. We were deluded (Eph. 2:2)
       1. The corrupting influence of "the world"

    2. The specific attitudes of "the world" (1 John 2:16)

    3. The passing nature of "the world"

C. We were dominated (Eph. 2:2)

    1. By the ruler of the kingdom of darkness

    2. By the spirit of disobedience

    3. By the cravings of sinful nature

D. We were doomed (Eph. 2:3)

    1. The wrath of God is real

    2. The wrath of God is holy

    3. The wrath of God is on us

II. The divine solution

A. The attitude from which it stems (Eph. 2:4–5)

    1. The love of God

    2. The mercy of God

    3. The grace of God

B. The means through which it comes—Christ is the answer

    1. From deadness to life

    2. From delusion to truth

    3. From domination to liberty

    4. From doom to the way back

C. The ways in which it works

    1. Grace—the initiative that provides it

    2. Faith—the humility that accepts it

    3. Works—the activity that demonstrates it

III. The personal reaction

A. You have been saved

B. You have not been saved

53

The Role of Women

The traditional role of women has been challenged in recent years in the Western world, and the resultant changes have produced much trauma. A biblical perspective needs to be maintained.

    I. Some background considerations
       A. The causes of change
          1. Emancipating developments
             a. Freedom from societal demands
             b. Freedom from sexual restrictions
          2. Educational opportunities
             a. Discovery of female competence
             b. Development of female expertise
          3. Economic considerations
             a. The double-income family lifestyle
             b. The single-parent family necessities
          4. Egalitarian concepts
             a. Militant approach to feminism
             b. Moderate approach to fairness
       B. The consequences of change
          1. Confusion about female identity

      a. Happy homemaker
      b. Cultured career girl
   2. Conflict between opposing positions
      a. Submitted and satisfied
      b. Free and frustrated
   3. Consternation about long-term possibilities
      a. Societal structures
      b. Individual development

II. Some biblical concepts
  A. Woman as a created being
    1. Created to be "man" (Gen. 1:26–30)
    2. Created to be female
      In relation to:
      a. Man (Gen. 2:20)
      b. Family (Gen. 4:1–2; Prov. 1:8)
      c. Home (1 Tim. 5:14)
      d. Society (Prov. 31:10–31)
  B. Woman as fallen being
    1. The generalities of fallen-ness
    2. The specifics of female fallen-ness (Gen. 3:16)
  C. Woman as redeemed being
    1. Woman's special place in redemption (e.g., Mary)
    2. Woman's complete enjoyment of redemption (Gal. 3:28)
    3. Woman's position in ministry of redemption (Acts 1:14; 2:17–21)

III. Some basic conclusions
  A. Anything that dehumanizes woman is unacceptable
    1. Sex kitten
    2. Kitchen slave

B. Anything that contravenes divine principle is untenable
    1. Denial of role
    2. Reversal of role
C. Anything that hinders God's purposes is inexcusable
    1. Frustration of gift
    2. Refusal of opportunity
D. Anything that gives Satan a toehold is unthinkable
    1. Tendency to schism
    2. Mishandling of issues

54

The Role of Men

B ut now, O LORD, thou art our Father, we are the clay, and thou our potter; and we all are the work of thy hand" (Isa. 64:8 KJV).

I. The Potter
   The Lord and Father (Isa. 43:10; Ps. 102:25; Gen. 1:7)
   A. The pot
      1. Dignified dust (Gen. 3:19)
      2. Marvelously made (Ps. 139:13–16)
   B. The person
      1. The spirit of man (Zech. 12:1)
   C. The plan
      1. On his mind (Ps. 139:1–3)
      2. In his book (v. 16)
   D. The problem
      1. The model marred (Jer. 18:1)
   E. The provision
      1. Christ (Heb. 10:5)

II. The purpose
  A. Partner with God (Gen. 1:28)
    1. Centered on the wheel (1 Cor. 11:3)
    2. Finished in the kiln (Rom. 5:3–5; Dan. 3)
  B. Protector of wife (Eph. 5:22–33)
    1. The composite arrangement (Ps. 68:6)
    2. Wet clay (1 Cor. 13:4–6)
  C. Parent of children (Eph. 6:4)
    1. Father–after his image (Matt. 5:48)
    2. Children–after our image (Phil. 3:12)

III. The Promise
  Bone China (Ps. 17:15)

Cassette tapes of the sermons preached from the outlines in this book are available from

TELLING THE TRUTH
P.O. Box 11
Brookfield, WI 53005